The magical adventure of littl~ Alf

By Hannah Russell

The Magical adventure of little Alf...

★★ Believe in magic and you will find it...

The discovery of the wild pony...

Book 1

***

Hannah has just moved to the North Yorkshire Dales. With a passion for horses, she starts riding at nearby Meadowlea Stables.

When she spots a small wild black pony one day whilst out trekking, in her heart Hannah finds herself determined to return and see him again. But what will happen if nobody believes she saw the pony? Will she give up all hope?

Embark on the magical adventure and follow Hannah as she enters the enchanted forest...

Chapter One

'Come on Hannah, get in the car' said Hannah's Mum.

'I'm coming Mum, I just need to find my riding boots and my hat.' They had just moved in to their new house in the Yorkshire Dales, and Hannah was going to the new stables for the first time. She was very nervous. Hannah had been very excited about moving. Her Mum and Dad had said that she would be able to be more responsible, and maybe get her own horse now that they were living in the country.

 Hannah found her riding hat and boots still in a box in the garage, her velvet hat still perfectly polished from when she had spent some hours cleaning it before boxing it up to move. Hannah ran to the car clutching hat and boots, all ready to head to the stables.

'Hannah what took you so long? You're going to be late for your lesson at this rate!' said Mum.

'I had to find my hat and boots Mum, I really don't want to be late, are we going to make it in time?' she asked.

Hannah's mum chuckled, 'Yes. I knew this would happen. That's why I left plenty of time so you could get ready.'

Hannah fastened her seatbelt and began to wonder what colour the pony she would be riding today would be, what his name might be, and whether he would like carrots or apples best. She had brought both with her just in case, and couldn't wait to get to the new stables. It seemed a long time since the last time she had been riding.

She was devastated to leave her old stables; she had made a special bond with a white pony called Star. She thought he was amazing, and he had taught Hannah to ride. Hannah's Mum and Dad had tried to buy Star for Hannah, but the owner would not sell him. Her Mum had been very worried about her when they had to move, as she knew Hannah loved Star very much, and wondered if she would ever again find the same bond with another horse.

'Think we're nearly here' said Hannah's Mum.

'I'm so excited! I wonder which horse I'll be riding, and if there will be any that look like Star' said Hannah.

Hannah admired the countryside as they started the journey up a steep winding hill. There were no houses in sight, just miles of fields, and sheep and cows in the distance. Hannah squinted her eyes; there was

something moving very fast across one of the fields. As the car moved further up the hill, she saw that the figure moving across the field was a horse!

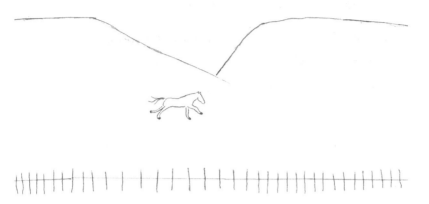

'Mum! Look!' she shouted.

Hannah's Mum laughed and shook her head, 'Horse mad you are.' She was glad to see Hannah being more like her old self. As they drove to the top of the hill, Hannah watched the horse move across the field. It was magical to her. When Hannah was little, her Mum and Dad used to take her to the beach to ride on the donkeys, and they both knew then that she would love horses when she was older. There was a warning sign for horses crossing the road so Hannah knew they were getting near to the stables.

'Look Mum, look! There's the sign for Meadowlea! Hannah shouted.

Her mum grinned 'Yes I think you're right.'

The car turned down the dusty track towards the stables. There were grass paddocks on either side of the worn dusty track. Hannah sat up in her seat looking for horses grazing in the paddocks but could not see any.

'Where are all the horses?' she wondered to herself. Her Mum pulled up outside a white cottage, which had WELCOME in big letters on its solid oak door.

Chapter Two

Hannah hopped out of the car with excitement, she could smell the grass of fresh meadows, and hear the low whinny of one of the horses. She knew she was going to love it here.

'Sit up straight, girls' a voice bellowed out, 'Move down the centre line'.

Hannah looked at her mum with confusion, 'Where's that voice coming from Mum?' she asked.

'It sounds like someone's having a riding lesson. Let's go see if we can find out' said Mum.

She wandered around the side of the building, admiring the red and pink roses which ran up the side of the pearl white cottage. As she moved around to the back, it was almost like a dream come true; Hannah stood watching in amazement. There were horses and ponies of all shapes, sizes and colours; she had never seen so many horses in one place. It was magical.

There were horses in wooden stables, people giggling and laughing, horses and ponies grazing in the lush green meadows, hanging baskets full of flowers in blossom, and, in the distance, Hannah could see a cross-country course set out across the fields.

'Wow! Mum, look! Look mum!' Hannah exclaimed. She could not believe all the different facilities at the stable. 'Think you're going to like it here then, Hannah?' her Mum asked.

'I love it already!' Hannah giggled with joy as she wandered down toward the wooden stables.

'Sit up straight Lily' the same voice shouted out.

Hannah looked across the yard to see where the mystery voice was coming from, and as she looked around she saw in the distance a golden sand ménage with horses walking, trotting and cantering around it. She stood and admired the view with amazement.

'Why don't we go watch the rest of the riding lesson Hannah?' suggested her Mum.

'Do you think we'll be allowed? I don't want to get into trouble on my first day!'

'Of course we are Hannah, Don't be shy, you might even be able to pick up some tips, and maybe even make new friends.'

Hannah nervously walked over to the brown wooden fence, and stood to watch the rest of the lesson, there were 10 different horses and ponies in the sand ménage, all different colours and sizes; Hannah was amazed at the way the horses and ponies responded, and hoped that one day she would have the ability to ride as well as the girls and boys having the lesson. Once the lesson had finished, the children dismounted and led the horses and ponies around the sand ménage to cool off.

'You must be Hannah' said the lady who had been teaching the girls and boys. Hannah smiled and nodded shyly. Her Mum laughed.

'She isn't usually this quiet! Hannah loves horses, but she seems to be a bit nervous about starting to ride somewhere new.'

'There's nothing to be worried about here Hannah. Our aim is to have lots of fun with the horses, and learn how to look after them correctly and give them the right care. My name's Ruth, and I've been teaching at Meadowlea Stables for three years; but I started riding here when I was just your age! I think you'll love it here, once you get settled in.'

Chapter Three

Ruth showed Hannah around the stables after her Mum had gone. Hannah was scheduled to have a riding lesson in the morning and then go out for an afternoon hack across the fields. She was fascinated by the stables; every stable door had a metal plaque on it with all the different horses names - Badger, Paddy, Pepper, Ryan, Teddy, Boy Dancer, King, Casper, Roadie, Timmy and more. Hannah smiled to herself; she had never seen stables as posh as this before!

Ruth smiled to herself. 'I recognise your expression' she said. Hannah looked at Ruth in confusion. 'What do you mean?' she asked.

'When I first started at Meadowlea Stables, I probably had the same expression on my face that you have now. I was so fascinated by everything; the beautiful stables, the smell of the leather in the tack room, the fresh smell of cut hay, and of course the sweet smell of the horses' said Ruth.

Hannah giggled 'I can't wait to ride, I love horses, and it's so nice here. I think I could live in one of those stables!'

Ruth laughed 'I think it would be very cold at night!'

'I think you could be right' laughed Hannah.

Ruth showed Hannah around the rest of the stables, and the old barn where she could put her packed lunch for the day.

'I think you've seen everything for now. How about I show you which pony you'll be riding for this morning's lesson?' said Ruth.

'Yes please!' Hannah said excitedly.

They walked back over to the stables, where the horses whinnied as they saw Hannah and Ruth approaching. Hannah giggled, 'I love it when horses whinny. What does it mean?'

'It can mean many different things, that they're happy to see you, they're greeting you, or maybe looking for a friend' said Ruth.

'I think they're happy to see you' said Hannah.

'I think they're happy to see us! They often get excited when they know they're going to get attention.' Ruth replied.

The sun was gleaming through the arched windows in the barn as Hannah and Ruth walked down past each stable. As they walked, the horses and ponies gently lifted their heads over the doors to greet them. Hannah gently stroked each horse's nose as she walked past.

'The fur on the horses feels like silk', Hannah thought to herself. 'So soft and gentle'.

'Hannah I would like you to meet Badger, he's the pony you'll be riding for this morning's lesson' Ruth explained.

Hannah gingerly tiptoed towards the stable, she was so excited to meet the horse she would be riding. As she drew near, the small pony lifted his chin over the stable. Hannah held her breath; he was gorgeous!

'Hello Badger' Hannah murmured, as she tickled his face. Badger snorted and shook his head with delight.

Badger was a Welsh Section C black and white cob, he had four white socks, perfectly rounded hooves, a white blaze down the front of his face and a long black shiny mane and tail. Hannah was amazed at how shiny he was, and could not wait to ride him in the ménage.

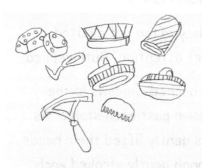

'First of all, Badger will need to be groomed and tacked up, his equipment is in the tack room, and also we need to make sure you have a securely fitted helmet and body protector to keep you safe' said Ruth.

Hannah nodded with excitement and went to gather Badger's tack from the tack room...

Once Hannah had tacked Badger up, she led him out to the sand ménage, where Ruth was waiting for Hannah to start the lesson.

'All ready?' Ruth asked.

'Yes. I can't wait!' Hannah replied.

Hannah led Badger towards the mounting block, pulled both

her stirrups down and checked the girth one last time, before stepping up and getting on. She slipped both her feet into the stirrups and gently picked up the reins.

'Remember not to hold your breath Hannah. Badger will look after you, just breathe as normal, there's nothing to be nervous about' said Ruth.

'I am a little nervous' admitted Hannah.

'Well don't worry, Badger is a gentle giant and he's taught so many people to ride, he's a professional by now! We're just going to do some simple walk/stop work to start with,' shouted Ruth from the centre of the ménage.

Hannah gently squeezed Badger 'Walk on' she instructed. Badger responded by walking forward around the edge of the ménage, and it wasn't long before Hannah was doing walk trot and canter transitions. She could not believe she was cantering around the ménage on her very first lesson at Meadowlea Stables! It wasn't long before Ruth was telling Hannah to walk Badger around the ménage and cool him down. Badger snorted and lowered his head as Hannah patted his neck. 'Good boy, Badger' she said.

'What did you think of your first lesson on Badger then Hannah?' said Ruth when it was over.

'It was fantastic! Badger is so good, and once I got used to his bouncy canter it felt amazing to be back riding again. I've missed it so much!' said Hannah.

'Yes he does have a bouncy canter, but once he gets going he's great, I'm surprised at how much you already knew about riding! You must have learnt a lot at your last riding school' said Ruth.

'Well, I rode a small pony called Star, he taught me loads' said Hannah.

'Ah that explains it then' said Ruth.

Hannah dismounted, and led Badger into his stable, the sun was beaming through the stable door, and Hannah smiled to herself as she removed Badger's tack and brushed him down. Hannah then went and got him the apple she had sliced at home earlier that morning. Hannah giggled as Badger stood and munched it.

'Do you like that, Badger?' Hannah asked as he snorted and shook his head.

'He's quite a character' said the girl who was leaning over Badger's stable door. Hannah jumped, and fell backwards into Badger's stable.

'I didn't mean to scare you' said the girl, trying not to giggle.

Hannah laughed 'I didn't see you standing there. You made me jump!'

'I could hear you talking to someone so I came to see who was in Badger's stable,' said the girl.

'I was just feeding him some apple I brought from home,' said Hannah.

'Badger likes apple! I usually bring the horses a carrot each when I come for my lessons,' said the girl.

'This is my first day at Meadowlea and I wasn't sure if the horses would like carrots or apples better, so I brought both' said Hannah.

'I thought I hadn't seen you around here before! My names Tilly! What's your name?' said the girl. Hannah giggled as she told Tilly her name.

'I think we're going to be great friends! We should have a riding lesson together one day! Or even go out hacking. I could show you all the bridleways,' said Tilly.

'That would be fun, I still haven't got used to the area since we moved house,' said Hannah.

'Well we will definitely go out riding then,' said Tilly.

'I can't wait!' Hannah replied.

'Which school will you be starting at?' asked Tilly.

'Mum's just enrolled me at Thorneberry Primary School' replied Hannah.

'That's fantastic! That's where I go! I'll introduce you to everyone, they're all really nice, and there's an old library behind Miss Alder's office which has the most fascinating stories and photos of horses. There's one special book which I'll show you; it's one of the oldest books in the library but has the most wonderful tips and tricks about how to ride and look after your very own horse,' said Tilly.

'That sounds great! I hope one day I will have my very own horse! Mum and Dad said that once we'd moved house it could be a possibility, but horses are a big responsibility so I'll just have to wait and see,' replied Hannah.

'Wow! You're so lucky that your parents are considering letting you have your very own horse! I would love to have my own horse, but I love riding Jack here at the stables,' said Tilly.

There was a loud beep of a car outside the stables; Badger pricked his ears.

'That must be Dad, I'd better go, see you soon!' shouted Tilly, as she skipped down the stables.

'She seemed nice' Hannah said to Badger as she patted him. Badger snorted and shook his head, before nuzzling Hannah's pockets for more treats.

Chapter Four

Hannah sat around a picnic bench with Ruth and the rest of the girls and boys who were going out on the afternoon hack across country. Hannah was very excited. She had only ever ridden in a sand ménage, as her old riding school was along a busy road and there was nowhere to hack out, as it was far too dangerous.

Ruth gave each of the riders a map of the route they would be taking 'Right team, this afternoon's hack will be across open fields, through the extraordinary mystical stream and the magical forest... I want you all to look after Hannah, as this is her first hack out with Meadowlea Stables and we want to show her a good time and really explore the area! Remember we want to have lots of fun out hacking, but the key thing is to be safe. It's a completely different environment to the ménage; but that doesn't mean we won't be cantering across the open fields at some point' said Ruth.

The group cheered, as Hannah laughed and chatted to the other girls and boys in the group.

'Why did Ruth call it the mystical stream and magical forest?' inquired Hannah to the redhaired girl sitting next to her.

'Well there are some old legends in the forest about magical horses that once roamed the land there, and in spring the stream turns turquoise in the sun and it makes the ride through the forest so magical. You'll love it, it's simply breathtaking. We were riding through the forest last summer and saw a herd of wild deer' said the redhaired girl.

'Wow!' said Hannah. Now she was really looking forward to going out hacking and visiting the forest. The group finished their lunch before being assigned to their horses for the afternoon. Hannah was riding a horse called Paddy for the hack. She couldn't believe her eyes when she saw him. He was magnificent. She squealed with joy; he was her dream horse. He was a bold affectionate Gypsy Cob, he had four black hooves covered in pearl white feathers; he stood up elegantly, looking trustworthy and high-spirited, and she could not wait to ride him...

Hannah was soon tacked up and ready to go with the rest of the group. She mounted Paddy and set off down the narrow dusty track with the group in single file. All the horses had a spring in their step as they headed down the lane. It wasn't long before Hannah understood why everybody loved riding across the country so much. 'Wow' she said to herself with amazement.

 She could see fields for miles and miles, an old rusty mill which was perched on the top of a steep hill surrounded by a luxurious turquoise blue lake. Some tractors were cutting fresh grass to make hay for the winter. 'It's spectacular!' she thought to herself.

Paddy's ears pricked up as Ruth rode up alongside Hannah.

'What do you think to riding through the country then, Hannah?'

'It's amazing. You notice so many more things when you're out hacking then when you're sitting in the car!'

'Yes you're right!' said Ruth.

'I hope that one day I will have my own horse and be able to ride across the country whenever I want to' said Hannah.

Ruth laughed 'There are certain rules about riding over somebody else's land, but as long as it's a bridleway and you have permission then you should be fine. We're going to have a little trot up the next field if you feel ready?'

'I certainly do!' grinned Hannah.

The group stopped while Ruth told everyone the plan. 'Right group, we'll be trotting up the next field; remember some of the horses will be a little excited. Just remind them that you're sitting on them, give them a gentle pat to let them know you're there, once we begin. I want you all to stay in single file on the track. Ready to go?' asked Ruth.

'Yes!' the whole group chirped back.

Hannah gathered up Paddy's reins. He snorted and swished his head with excitement. 'Steady boy' she said, as she gently patted his neck.

The whole group set off up the track, while Hannah trotted at the back of the group. She was nervous to start with but soon settled into Paddy's fast trot, his silky black mane flowing in the wind. She couldn't believe she was trotting across an open field. Paddy seemed to love trotting, his ears were pricked and his head was set on line as he followed the rest of the group up the track.

It wasn't long before Hannah could see a small group of trees in the distance; all the horses started to prance and swish their tails in excitement. She realized she was approaching the magical forest Ruth and the redhaired girl had mentioned earlier...

As they approached the wood, there was a large oak bridge, which was covered in rose pink blossom. The horses began to steadily move across the solid oak bridge, leaving a trace of hoof prints as they moved across.

'Remember to reassure the horses as you cross the bridge. It is unusual ground for them so we want to let them know it's okay,' called Ruth from the front of the group.

Paddy hesitated as he stepped both feet onto the bridge; his nostrils flared and his eyes widened as he lowered his head and snorted. 'It's okay Paddy' said Hannah as she gently stroked his neck. Hannah squeezed him with her thighs to encourage him to walk over the bridge, she allowed him to take the reins as he gingerly tiptoed over the bridge. 'It's okay' Hannah repeated in a soothing voice and it wasn't long before they had crossed. Paddy swished his head and sighed in delight. 'Well done Paddy' said Hannah as she patted his neck.

'Right team, we are now in the magical forest, be aware the surrounding is more enclosed, and although the horses have been here before, there are different sounds than usual.

There'll be a short section to canter before cooling the horses down in the stream, and there'll also be small jumps which you can have a go at one by one, if you feel up for it! Everybody ready?' shouted Ruth.

The group cheered, and began to walk the horses on. The silvery twigs rustled on the trees as the wind passed through the forest. The sun shone through the green leaves, creating shadows beneath the horses' feet. The ground seemed to be damp and trodden as the horses wandered through the forest. There was a smell of moist earth.

As Hannah and Paddy walked there seemed to be a glimmer of shining silver dust in the air, 'This really is magic...' said Hannah as she gently stroked him.

It was just at that moment that Hannah saw something move out of the corner of her eye. Something small and very dark...

Chapter Five

Paddy's head shot up, his ears pricked, his nostrils flared, and his entire body became bolt upright. It soon became apparent that it wasn't just Hannah who had seen the creature. Paddy began to prance on the spot.

'Steady boy' Hannah cried, Paddy spun round on the spot, looking for the creature he had seen. Hannah could hear Ruth shouting in the distance, but it all became a blur, it was happening too quick. Hannah panicked, she kicked Paddy in fright as he came to a dead stop. He was breathing heavily as he looked around. Hannah let out a huge gasp, she had been holding her breath the entire time. Hannah scanned the scenery. What was it that they had just seen...?

Ruth came trotting down from the front of the ride, 'Are you okay? What happened?' Ruth asked.

Hannah looked at Ruth in shock 'I.. I.. I think so' she stuttered.

'You seem a bit shaken, are you sure you are okay?' Ruth said.

'I saw something, something small in the woods. I think Paddy saw it too, that's why he was so frightened' said Hannah.

'It's not like Paddy to get frightened easily, it must have been a deer lurking in one of the trees.' said Ruth.

'No it was much smaller, and so dark, almost black, it looked fluffy, but I'm not sure, it all happened so quickly' said Hannah.

'Hmmm, well we certainly don't get bears in our country, so I'm not sure what it could have been, maybe a badger? They're often found in the woods' said Ruth.

'I don't think so' said Hannah.

'Well at least Paddy seems to have calmed down now, do you think you'll be okay to ride him back to the stables?' asked Ruth.

'Of course. He's so sweet. He just got frightened. I thought you mentioned a canter anyway?' said Hannah.

Ruth laughed 'We'd better carry on through the forest then. If you want you can come ride up front with me to give Paddy more reassurance' said Ruth.

As they trotted up to the front of the ride, Hannah couldn't help but wonder what it was they had seen. She was certain it wasn't a badger...

It wasn't long before Hannah and the rest of the group came across a small archway which had been formed by the forest trees. Through the small archway was a brown dusty track which had a scattering of blue flowers. There was a ray of sun shining through a gap in the trees, and a faint sound of running water, almost as if a tap was trickling. All the horses came to a sudden halt.

'This is my favourite place' said one of the brown-haired boys who was sitting on a brown appaloosa. 'Yours too, isn't it boy' he said, patting the horse.

'Well it looks like the horses know where we are' said Ruth'

Paddy shook his head in excitement, 'Where are we, boy?' Hannah asked, giving Paddy a pat.

'We're near the mysterious stream' Ruth explained. 'Once you go through the archway there's a small stream which runs right in front of you. The horses have to go through it to get to the other side of the forest, it's lots of fun! And on the other side is a small cross country course'.

'I can't wait, I wonder what colour the stream will be this time of the year' said the red haired girl Hannah had been talking to at lunch.

'That sounds wonderful, and so exciting' said Hannah as she looked through the naturally formed archway.

'Right team, most of you are aware we have to go single file through the archway, then, once we reach the stream, remain in single file, it is a matter of your pony trusting you as you go through the stream, as they are not sure what's underneath them. It's up to you as riders to encourage your pony through, which means plenty of reassurance! Once we're through we can proceed to the cross-country course, all sound okay?' shouted Ruth to the group.

'Yes!' everyone shouted back.

'Let's go then' Ruth replied.

Hannah could feel a buzz through her body. She couldn't wait to try some of the jumps. She had never been over a cross-country course before. Paddy walked eagerly through  the forest arch, and the blue flower petals swished along the dusty track as his feathered tail brushed by. His ears pricked as a rabbit hopped over the track in front of him and the noise of running water became increasingly louder.

Then, through a long twisted branch, Hannah saw the mysterious stream....

***

It was narrow, no wider than a stable door... but there was something different about this stream. There was a silver tinge in the moss which was covering the gold stones, there were long vines running either side of the stream where rose- coloured flowers bloomed. It was like a fairy palace. Paddy gingerly tiptoed to the water's edge, stepping one hoof forward at a time. The water flowed around his feathers, elegantly travelling down the stream, shimmering shades of violet and blue.

Paddy lowered his head and snorted at the water trickling by, 'It's alright, Paddy' Hannah said as she squeezed her legs around him. Paddy slowly, and very tentatively, stepped forward, before leaping onto the grassy bank. 'Well done Paddy!' Hannah said, laughing. Paddy snorted and swished his head.

'Well that's one way to get to the other side!' said Ruth. The whole group laughed and carried on walking up the field towards the cross- country jumps.

Chapter Six

'We can do this, Paddy' Hannah said as she headed for her first jump. Paddy's feet hammered on the dry grass field, creating hoofmarks as they cantered up the grassy bank.

The first cross-country jump was quite small and rather wide, but Hannah was nervous as Paddy headed in towards the

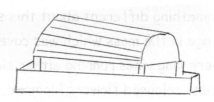

middle of it in a steady canter. She held her breath as his body rose gracefully, skimming the grassy edge of the jump. He landed elegantly at the other side, placing each hoof to the floor effortlessly.

'Phew, that was amazing!' cried Hannah, as she let out a huge sigh of breath. She was thrilled at jumping her very first cross-country jump with a pony like Paddy.

'Right team, can you all gather round here please' shouted Ruth, standing by a hedge which had been formed in to one of the higher jumps. The group trotted over.

'Right. Is everybody okay?' asked Ruth.

'Yes!' the group excitedly chirped back.

'Right then, we're going to discuss jumping before we set off around the course, so the important things when jumping are to keep your heels down in the stirrups and let your hands go forward as you take off. I noticed a few of you were pulling back slightly and the aim is to glide over the jump with your horse so you look collected. This also allows your horse to jump more easily, and makes sure you're not giving him a wrong signal when going over the jump. Do we all feel happy with that, and ready to give the course a go?' said Ruth.

'Yes!' the group shouted again, and Hannah giggled excitedly.

Grace, a thin blonde-haired girl was first to go over the course. Hannah and the rest of the group gathered underneath an old oak tree while they stood and watched her gracefully tackle each jump. As Grace landed each jump effortlessly on the grey horse, Hannah was amazed and hoped one day she would be able to fly over the course in the same way.

'Well done Grace' Ruth shouted as she finished elegantly.

'That was amazing' Hannah said out loud.

'That grey horse and Grace have been a great partnership for years; they're hard to beat in show season, they have such a strong bond,' said blond-haired Bobbie.

'Right Hannah, you're up' said Ruth.

'Let's go' Hannah said as she squeezed her legs around Paddy. His head rose from the dozy position he had been standing in underneath the oak tree, and he began to jig-jog excitedly towards the cross country course. 'Good boy' Hannah said, patting him as he snorted.

Hannah paid attention to the first jump, looking around and planning it before they got there. She squeezed Paddy into trot, and then pushed him on to the canter. His ears pricked forward as they headed towards the first jump. His hooves glided across the ground as he got nearer, and Hannah grinned as she knew she was going to make the jump. She moved herself into jumping position and wrapped her legs around Paddy to encourage him to take off early so he wouldn't bang the wood with his hooves. As he lifted his body into the air, Hannah felt like she was flying. He landed at the other side with ease, and cantered on to the next jump.

'Good boy!' Hannah cried, as she patted him. Paddy leapt forward with a small buck of excitement. Hannah giggled and headed straight for the second jump, which was much narrower and a few inches higher than the last one. Hannah set Paddy on straight and aimed for the middle of the jump. With his ears pricked and eyes brightened, he changed his stride to a steadier pace.

'It's okay, we can do this' Hannah said in a soothing voice, as the coloured pony switched his ears back to listen to Hannah as they took off for the jump. Paddy's hooves skimmed the wooden bark as they landed on the other side.

'Not quite as graceful, but at least we landed it' Hannah thought as they cantered towards the third jump.

This one was different from all the other jumps, high on one side and lower on the other. Ruth had explained earlier that the third fence was the most difficult one in the course, and was called a drop fence, meaning that they would land at a lower level then the one they jumped from. Hannah began to understand the risks as they got nearer to it.

She headed straight for the fence, easing Paddy into a faster stride, but not letting go contact on the rein. Hannah knew if they kept like this they would sail over the jump with no problem and be able to complete the course. She wrapped her legs around Paddy as he took off over the jump too early. She braced herself for the other side...

It was a tense moment. Hannah felt like she was in the air a long time before they landed; she adjusted her seat and sat back knowing she would need all the support she could get as Paddy landed with a thud. As Hannah bounced about in the saddle landing on Paddy's neck as he thrived forward, she had seconds to balance herself before the fourth jump.

Sitting up in her stirrup irons, she grabbed hold of Paddy's mane, knowing she had no time to regain her rein contact. Hannah and Paddy leapt over the fourth jump; slightly unbalanced, but they cleared it. 'Good boy!' Hannah patted

Paddy, knowing that he had looked after her over that last jump. She knew if she had been riding any other horse she could have been thrown off.

They headed up towards the fifth and final jump in the course. It was large, and had been formed out of the stump of an old tree. 'Easy'. Hannah tickled Paddy's neck. She set him online and headed towards the middle of the jump, just as she saw something move out of the corner of her eye. Something small and very fast was moving alongside of them...

Chapter Seven

Paddy burst into a flat out gallop, going as fast as he could across the open field. He swerved the fifth jump by inches, his ears twitched as he scanned the area. Hannah realised it was the same creature she had seen earlier, and was determined to find out what upset Paddy...

'It's okay' Hannah cried shakily, wondering if she was trying to convince herself or Paddy as he moved towards the forest.

'Use your brakes!' she heard Ruth call as she cantered up from behind. Hannah pulled on Paddy's reins 'Whoa boy!' she cried, but Paddy had other ideas. He surged forwards, his ears pinned back in fright. Hannah now knew there was something out there, but what was it? She looked around trying to find answers but could only see the trees and the undergrowth moving. 'How small is this creature? Hannah thought to herself. It's as if it was invisible'.

Hannah pulled Paddy towards the nearby trees trying to move him off track in a last bid to slow him down. Hannah could feel Paddy becoming tired as he began to slow down to a steady canter. She could still see something moving out of the corner of her eye. Paddy came to an abrupt stop; his eyes widened as the hedge rattled.

He arched his head forward and snorted at the hedge, before swinging his quarters in towards it, still thinking he was in danger.

There was a sudden low howling sound, almost like a whinny but Hannah wasn't sure, it sounded so quiet and muffled, was it the wind moving the trees, or was there something in the hedge? Paddy suddenly let out a gentle whinny calling to whatever it was that was underneath the trees.

'Paddy can gallop, that's for sure!' panted Ruth as she came up beside Hannah, on the grey horse. 'I even had to borrow Grace's horse to try and keep up with him!' said Ruth.

'He's been frightened by something in the woods! I'm pretty sure it was the same animal as earlier, I definitely saw something move out of the corner of my eye as we headed towards the final jump. It was just like earlier but this time Paddy took flight and I'm pretty sure whatever it was can move pretty fast, and I'm almost certain it whinnied at me and Paddy' said Hannah half excited, half scared. Ruth looked at Hannah incredulously.

'Well..ermm..' she said, staggering as she spoke.

'I honestly saw something moving, it looked dark and small just like the first time. I'm certain there's something out there in the woods' said Hannah, hoping that Ruth would believe her.

'Well I can mention it to the farmer, it may be a loose dog or maybe one of his sheep has escaped' said Ruth.

Hannah knew that whatever it was she was more determined than ever to find out, or Ruth would never believe her.

'Come on then. We'd better head back down to the rest of the group' said Ruth.

As Hannah and Ruth turned around to head back, Hannah saw something in the distance. Squinting her eyes against the sun, searching for answers, far away but with the sun distorting her vision, Hannah felt sure she had just seen a very small dark pony...

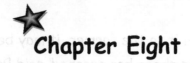

Chapter Eight

Meadowlea Stables looked different as the group steadily headed up the dusty track, the sun setting behind the white cottage, creating a shimmering glow of light

around the old rusty barn, the horses gently grazing   in the field, contentedly swishing their tails as the night drew on.

'This is so peaceful' Hannah thought to herself as she headed into the yard with Paddy. She slid reluctantly off him before wrapping her arms around his neck and hugging him tightly. 'Thank you so much Paddy, we've had the best day ever' said Hannah as she squeezed him one last time.

Paddy snorted and nudged Hannah's pocket, 'Okay, you can

have the carrots now!' Hannah giggled as she gave him the carrots from her pockets. Hannah saw the black BMW pull in to Meadowlea as her Mum arrived.

'Looks like its home time' sighed Hannah as she patted Paddy. She untacked him and led him into his stable.

'Have you had a good day then?' asked Hannah's Mum as she leaned over the stable door.

'It's been fantastic! I rode a black and white cob called Badger this morning in the ménage, we practiced walk, trot and canter work, it was so much fun! Can you believe I was cantering? And then this afternoon I went out on Paddy across to the magical forest and over the mystical stream! It was so much fun, we even got to go over cross-country jumps, but the best part of it was I think there's a wild black pony living in the woods. I only saw it as we turned around to come home, but it was definitely a horse Mum, it was so tiny too, I've never seen a horse so small!' Hannah gabbled excitedly.

'Well that does sound like a full day, are you sure it was a pony, Hannah?' asked Hannah's mum.

'Well to start with I thought I was just being silly, but Paddy saw it too, and at the end I had a clear view across the fields and I don't know any other animal which has a mane, tail and hooves, do you, Mum?'

'Well that does sound like a horse to me. Did anyone else see it?' Hannah's mum asked.

Ruth came round the corner with her two Labradors by her side.

'We had a good day didn't we Hannah!'

'Yes it's been fantastic, I couldn't believe how wonderful it was, and the best part was I think I saw a wild horse!' Hannah replied.

Ruth looked at Hannah worriedly, before glancing back to Hannah's Mum.

'Right I think we'd better be going now Hannah, your Dad will be on his way back from work and I have to get tea ready' said Hannah's Mum.

'Okay then' Hannah sighed as she hugged Paddy one last time.

'Well it's been nice meeting you Hannah, will you be back again?' asked Ruth.

'Of course I will! I can't wait!' Hannah said.

Hannah and her mum hopped into the car, and headed back down the lane towards home. She was knocked over by their big golden and black German Shepherd as they walked into their new house.

'Hello Sasha' Hannah giggled as she stroked her. Sasha was two years old with big soft brown eyes and a thick silky coat, and she adored Hannah.

'Hello Hannah!' shouted her Dad from the lounge.

Hannah wandered through the hallway to join him. She still couldn't get her head round living somewhere new, it was so  different from the old house. The new house had a big solid oak beam above the fire place and there was a curved archway carved with elegant roses which gracefully moulded into the garden room. 'I love it here' Hannah thought to herself as she watched her dad unpack the last of the boxes.

'How was your horse riding day?' he asked.

'It was wonderful Dad! I can't wait to go back, best day of my life, and I saw a little wild pony in the magical forest! It was so small, I've never seen anything like it before'.

'Well that does sound like magic Hannah, sure it wasn't something else, like a bear?' asked Hannah's Dad.

Hannah giggled 'Dad don't be silly we don't get bears in the Yorkshire Dales, although it was very fluffy.'

Hannah's Dad grinned, 'So what type of horse did you ride today then?'

Hannah began to explain about her magical day at Meadowlea Stables…

She started her new school the following Monday. She was very nervous at first but managed to make lots of new friends. Although she was enjoying it, Hannah couldn't get the little pony she saw out of her mind. She knew nobody believed her, and she was almost starting to doubt herself, but her heart told her different. She knew she had seen something and was determined to find out more. She couldn't wait to get back to Meadowlea at the weekend. Hannah had met Tilly from the stables on her first day at school, and they talked endlessly about horses, and agreed to go out riding together that weekend. Hannah couldn't wait.

***

It was a sunny day without a cloud in the sky when Hannah woke up the following Saturday morning. She had excited butterflies in her tummy, because today she would be entering the magical forest once again. The week seemed to have dragged on and on and all Hannah wanted to do was go riding, and search for the little pony. She hurriedly threw on her pink patterned jodhpurs and crisp white polo top before belting downstairs.

'Morning Mum!' she chirped.

'Well you seem bright and cheery this morning!' her Mum laughed.

'Well I have an exciting day ahead of me! What time do we need to set off?' asked Hannah.

'Set off where?' questioned Mum.

'To the stables of course?' said Hannah worriedly.

'I'm only joking, we'll set off in ten minutes, let me quickly walk the dogs and get your brother out of bed'.

'Yippppeee!' cried Hannah, as she patted Maggie the golden  Cocker Spaniel. Quickly grabbing her riding hat and boots, Hannah began to wonder what would happen if she found the little pony, how would she catch it? Would it follow her willingly, or was it completely wild? Hannah grabbed her rucksack and went to the fridge, filling it with apples and carrots.

'I sure do hope it likes carrots!' Hannah murmured to herself.

'Are you talking to yourself again, Hannah?' teased her brother, John.

Hannah stuck her tongue out at him before bolting out of the front door. She jumped out of the car as soon as they reached Meadowlea Stables; the horses whinnied from the paddocks as they grazed the summer grass. Hannah saw Tilly brushing Jack as she leapt around the stable entrance. Jack was a black and white stocky cob with spectacular markings on his face and speckles of black running down his white blaze, which was very unique for a piebald. Jack had a defined muscular body from all the hard work Tilly had put in show jumping him through the summer. It was clear Tilly's love for Jack was mutual as he nuzzled her pockets and playfully tugged at her jumper.

'Hannah!' Tilly cried out with excitement as she saw Hannah approaching.

'Good morning!' Hannah giggled as Tilly hugged her.

'Are you excited about riding today? I can't wait, I hope I get to see the little pony' said Tilly. Hannah had told Tilly about the pony, figuring she needed all the help she could get.

'I hope we do too' sighed Hannah.

'It has to be around somewhere, we just have to look and be prepared for an adventure' said Tilly excitedly.

'You're right! I've packed a rucksack full of carrots and apples, I also have a torch, a head collar and lead rope and of course Smartie flavoured cookies for us!' said Hannah joyfully.

'Great! I love those!' said Tilly.

Hannah giggled as she went to find Ruth to ask which horse she would be riding today. She found her leading her little boy Ben around the ménage on a big brown and white skewbald stocky cob called Hovis. Hovis was taking very small steps, and looked like a very strong noble horse. His ears pricked as Hannah drew closer. Ruth saw Hannah steadily moving towards the ménage not wanting to frighten the skewbald.

 'Morning Hannah, I'll be with you in a minute' Ruth cried as she led Ben and Hovis around the ménage one last time.

Hannah took a seat on the blue bench next to the ménage, the bench was rusty and old with paint chipped away at each corner, and the iron rails, once silver, were now brown.

'Wouldn't sit on there if I were you' said the tall blonde-haired man standing next to Hannah. 'I've been so busy lately with work, and looking after Ben on Saturdays when Ruth works I haven't had time to fix it up yet'.

Hannah stood up, as Ruth's two Labradors came bounding round the corner. 'I'll make a rider out of him yet' said Ruth as she gently slid the little boy out of the saddle and handed him to the tall blonde haired man. 'I've put Ben's medicine on the table in the kitchen' Ruth told him.

Hannah looked confused. 'Ah yes, sorry Hannah. This is my husband Will and our little boy Ben, he's been a little poorly recently so we have to look after him and keep him wrapped up' said Ruth.

'Well that makes more sense now' giggled Hannah as she pulled a funny face at Ben.

Hannah and Ruth walked back to the stables as Ruth led Hovis. Hannah asked which horse she would be riding today.

'I think we should put you on Orky today, Hannah. He is a little bigger than the ponies you usually ride, but he's a gentle soul, he sometimes isn't great when you apply too much contact to the mouth, but when you're out hacking with Tilly he'll be great. Also if you do attempt any small jumps it's best to trot into them, He used to be a racehorse and he sometimes wants to gallop over them, but he'll always put the rider first, he's a very noble soul' said Ruth.

'I've only ever ridden ponies though.' Hannah said nervously.

'Don't worry! You're a good little rider and you'll handle Orky fine! Sometimes ponies can be a lot cheekier than horses' Ruth said.

Hannah headed round the stables in search of Orky. As she reached the stable door, she saw that Orky wasn't in his stable. She began to panic until Ruth shouted 'Orky's in the front paddock. He doesn't like the stable too much after his racing days.'

Hannah grabbed the black and gold head collar. As she drew nearer to the paddock she saw the big athletic looking thoroughbred. 'Wow' Hannah said as she breathed out. Orky flicked his head and whinnied as Hannah opened the gate. 'Hello, boy' Hannah said as she rubbed his forehead. Orky was a bay thoroughbred. He had a white snip and lip mark and a small white star in the centre of his forehead. His mane, tail and legs from the knees and hocks down were black. He was magnificent, and had a spring in his step as she led him to his stable.

After Hannah and Tilly had both tacked up and mounted, Ruth gave them a brief talk. 'Don't go off the track, and stay safe, remember to ring me if you have any problems and never put yourself in danger, okay?' said Ruth.

'Yes' the two girls chirped back.

As the two girls headed up the lane she could hear the chat among the two about the small black wild pony Hannah claimed to have seen the previous weekend. 'Typical' Ruth thought to herself, she thought that Hannah might have forgotten about the little pony, but knew if she was Hannah's age she would be just as determined to find out if the wild pony was real...

Chapter Nine

By late morning the sun was beating down furiously. Hannah and Tilly laughed as they headed up towards the forest entrance. Hannah had butterflies in her tummy again, anxious to find out if the little wild pony was still there. Orky seemed to sense Hannah's excitement, and pranced nervously up towards the wooden bridge.

As they went deeper into the forest, they could hear voices coming from in between the trees. 'I wonder who that could be?' Hannah thought to herself. They were soon met by a large Dapple grey thoroughbred ridden by a lady.

'Hello girls. Nice day!' said the lady.

'It sure is' chirped Tilly.

Once the lady had carried on down the track with her horse, Hannah asked Tilly who she was.

'Oh that's Diane, her nick name is Rusty, her horse is called Ryan. He used to be a very good racehorse; he won the Grand National a few years ago, and now she does cross-country courses with him. She was probably practising some jumps across the course' said Tilly.

'Wow. Mustn't she have had to retrain him?' questioned Hannah.

'She has her own yard, Colliwath stables it's called, it's not too far away from your new house. She takes in retired racehorses, retrains them and takes them in to rest them from all the big yards. It's amazing, the work they do' said Tilly passionately.

'They must be really good' said Hannah.

'Yes they did a series on TV last year about the yard' said Tilly.

'I wonder if Rusty has ever seen the little black pony' Hannah said to herself.

As they headed further into the forest, Hannah felt the magic of the branches once again around her, the flowers blossoming, and the dust glimmering against the light, creating silver dust around the trees. 'Pure magic.' Hannah thought to herself.

Hannah and Tilly trotted through the forest, Orky slipping on the damp ground. Hannah steadied him to a slower trot, before reassuring him to carry on. They kept their eyes peeled for the little black pony, but after endless searching along the track it was becoming apparent he was nowhere to be seen.

'This is no use' Hannah muttered, her eyes suddenly beginning to water a little. She was frustrated; last week she had spotted the little wild pony twice, and today the forest was quiet and the only movement was the pheasants beneath the leaves.

'Don't give up Hannah. Remember you said it is very small, we're probably just looking in the wrong place. This forest is huge, it could be anywhere! Anyway it isn't going to come on the track where we are, maybe we should split up?' suggested Tilly, patting Jack.

'Hmm... well we would have more chance to find it wouldn't we' said Hannah, as Orky snorted.

'Certainly would' replied Tilly.

Hannah and Tilly parted at the end of the forest, Hannah was slightly nervous remembering that Ruth had told the girls not to go off the track, but Hannah knew it was their only hope. She turned Orky to step off track. Orky was hesitant at first but soon eager to know where Hannah was taking him.

She patted his sleek neck and breathed in the woodland around her. 'Please be around here somewhere, please' Hannah whispered to herself, desperate to find the little pony. Orky's ears pricked up as they headed further down into the woodland; it was different off the track, the birds were singing, and the trees glistering with tiny drops of rain

which slid off the green leaves and splashed onto Orky's arched neck. Hannah urged him into a determined trot; he responded quickly, raising his poll and surging forwards.

'Steady boy' Hannah said stroking him gently. There was a large broken down tree stopping them in their tracks. 'Looks like we're going to have to turn round then, boy' Hannah sighed, wondering if it might all just be a dream. Hannah was just turning Orky around when she saw something move out of the corner of her eye. She knew it was the little wild pony...

Whipping Orky back round in the blink of an eye, she kicked him on to canter towards the broken down tree. Orky was hesitant but Hannah kicked him again. She was not going to miss this chance. Orky lifted his front feet, and Hannah sat up in her saddle as they sailed over the jump. She smiled and praised him, before half-halting him and bringing him back down to a steady walk. Orky's nostrils flared as the hedge rattled in front of them. He began to prance on the spot. Hannah held her breath as the little wild pony emerged from behind the hedge...

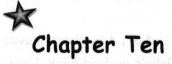

Chapter Ten

Orky stood bolt upright, not sure what to make of the little pony, Hannah couldn't believe her eyes. He was the smallest pony she had ever seen, she had seen miniature Shetlands before, but this little pony was far smaller.

She gently swung her leg over Orky and dismounted. Crouching down to the little pony's level, she tried to get a view of his eyes, which were covered by a brown fuzz of hair. He had four black stocks, and a unique chestnut brown fluffy coat almost like a little bear with a big fuzzy mane the colour of browns and Arubans, almost as if he had highlights! He had a long tail similar to his mane and the softest eyes Hannah had ever seen.

She gently held her hand out to the little pony, wanting to feel his soft fuzzy coat, the little pony hesitated and took a step back. Hannah remained in the same position, and gently got a carrot from her coat pocket, before offering it to the little pony. He slowly stepped forward and softly sniffed the carrot before taking the tiniest bite. Hannah's eyes brimmed with tears; she was so happy and, flooded with relief, she knew now it had not all been a dream.

The little pony whinnied at Orky who had been standing patiently behind Hannah the whole time. Hannah's heart almost burst with love for the little pony 'You are just too cute, aren't you!' Hannah said as she gently stroked him. 'This really is magic' Hannah thought to herself.

She knew she had to take the little pony back to Meadowlea Stables; she had to prove to everyone that he was real, but

 she was more concerned about the little pony's overgrown hooves, and noticed he had patches of fur missing from his belly which looked sore and in need of attention. She slowly crept around to her rucksack to get the head collar she had packed earlier, praying it would fit the little pony's tiny head.

She gently held out another carrot towards him; he didn't hesitate this time and took a big bite of the carrot before happily munching it. Hannah softly patted his neck as she slipped the lead rope around it. 'Just one last buckle' Hannah thought, slipping the buckle through the head collar.

'Hannah where are you?' shouted Tilly.

The little pony reared and lunged forward, taking Hannah with him. She was determined not to let go; she must take him back.

'Haa-n-aah!' Tilly shouted again.

The little pony bucked and reared, his nostrils flaring as his head collar buckle slipped the last notch and fell to the ground. He galloped off into the woods.

'No-oo! Come back!' Hannah cried, tears in her eyes. She was so close.

'There you are Hannah! I've been looking everywhere for you. Jack's getting tired and I think it's about time we headed back' said Tilly.

'I was so, so close' Hannah sobbed.

Tilly looked at Hannah, covered from head to toe in mud, with the head collar in her hand and tears streaming down her face, looking back into the woods.

'Whatever happened Hannah, are you okay?' asked Tilly.

'It was the little pony, I touched him, he's real. I was so close, but then you shouted. He got too scared and ran off!' Hannah said as tears began to stream even faster down her face.

'Oh Hannah, I am so sorry, I hadn't seen the little pony all day and I never thought you would actually find him. I was beginning to give up hope. Oh I'm so sorry. Would you like to go look for him again?'

'There's no point, he's scared now' Hannah said, frustrated, as she gathered Orky's reins back up before mounting.

Tilly glanced at Hannah worriedly then looked around the woodland. 'There's no evidence that the little pony has been around. Did she actually see him?' Tilly wondered to herself.

'Please say you believe me. Nobody else does' Hannah said between sobs.

'Of course I do' Tilly said, not sure what else she could say.

'I know what, why don't we leave a trail of carrots then if the little pony does come back, he might follow the carrots and come back to the stables?' Tilly said, trying to make Hannah feel better.

'Do you think it'll work?' asked Hannah.

'We can give it a go, right?' Tilly said enthusiastically.

Hannah began to spread the carrots on the way back to the stables, hoping Tilly was right. She knew Tilly had a good heart and was only trying to make her feel better, but how was a little pony ever going to follow a trail of carrots?

'This isn't a fairy tale' Hannah thought to herself, but didn't see any other option. Would she ever see the little pony again or should she just give up? Hannah slumped in the saddle and felt tears leak out from under her eyelids and run down her cheeks dripping on to Orky's shoulder as they rode back.

Ruth saw the two girls calmly walking into the stable yard. The horses looked happy and content, apart from the swishing of their tails as they tried to protect themselves from the evening flies. It was as they got nearer that Ruth saw something was very wrong. Hannah's face was streaked with tears and Tilly's expression was uncomfortable and worried.

'Girls! What happened, are you both okay?' Ruth said rushing over to them.

Hannah nodded and dismounted as she ran up his stirrups and gave him a carrot from her pocket. Ruth glanced at Hannah worriedly before looking at Tilly for some answers.

'We decided to go off track and look for the little pony. So we split up and then Hannah saw him, but I scared him away.' Tilly muttered.

Hannah heard Ruth gasp. She had told both of the girls to stay on the track, as the ground was too dangerous for the horses to go across.

'You could both have been seriously hurt; there is a reason you have to stick to the bridleway. It's against the rules to go off track, and people set all sorts of traps in the woods. Any horse or rider could get hurt out there, that's why a safe protective track is put in place to minimise any injuries'.

Hannah's eyes widened. She couldn't stand the thought of the little wild pony getting hurt or trapped. Everything else Ruth said after that seemed to be a muffle to Hannah, she was worried about the poor wild pony getting hurt, and once again nobody believed her.

It wasn't long before Hannah and Tilly's parents arrived, and they were soon going through the same lecture all over again.

*****

Hannah went to bed that night worn out. She didn't know how she was going to face school the next day. Her Mum and Dad had grounded her for a month for putting herself in danger. She knew they only cared about her but she couldn't take her mind off the little pony. Hannah also knew that her parents still didn't believe her, and repeatedly asked her if she was making up stories, but it was only Hannah that really knew, and she was still more determined than ever to find him.

As she lay in bed that night she kept thinking about what would have happened if Tilly hadn't shown up, things might have been different, the little wild pony could have been in a comfortable stable munching hay, or even in one of the small paddocks grazing the grass. Hannah sighed and shut her eyes. She fell asleep thinking about the little wild pony.

Chapter Eleven

The rain was belting down against the windowpanes the next morning, Hannah lay in bed listening to the faint splattering sounds coming from outside. There was a large bang as lightning struck the sky, and she shuddered underneath the covers. Hannah thought about the little pony as the rain began to hammer faster and faster against the windows. Would he be okay?

Eventually she got out of bed and dressed for school. She briefly heard the telephone ringing and glanced at the clock. 7:00 am. Who would be ringing at that time? She crept downstairs and heard her parents talking in the kitchen.

'I think we should take her to Meadowlea Stables this morning' said Hannah's Dad.

'No I don't think that's a good idea, let her go to school and we'll see after that' said Hannah's Mum.

'Yes, you're right. We don't want her falling behind in her classes' sighed her Dad.

Hannah gasped. What where they talking about? 'They can't ban me from Meadowlea'. Her eyes began to brim with tears.

***

The day was still grey as the final bell rang for school, Hannah slowly gathered up her things, and walked with Tilly across the school playground.

'I think Mum and Dad are going to ban me from the stables' Hannah whispered to Tilly, as she hung her head and looked at the ground.

'Don't be silly, that would be ridiculous! Who would I ride with anyway? They won't ban you, they know how much you love riding' Tilly said smiling at Hannah.

'Hmmm, maybe' Hannah faintly smiled at Tilly before sloping off to the car where her Mum and Dad were waiting for her.

'Good day at school, Hannah?' her Dad asked as she hopped into the car.

'It was okay.' Hannah muttered as Sasha began to smother her in kisses.

Hannah's Mum and Dad glanced at each other. It wasn't long before Hannah realized they weren't heading in the direction of home.

'Where we going?' she asked.

'We're just going to pick up some things.' Mum said as she glanced at her in the rear view mirror.

Hannah soon recognised the windy track they were

heading up and saw the signs for Meadowlea Stables. 'Where exactly are we picking up these things from?' Hannah asked.

Hannah's parents grinned at each other and carried on driving up towards the stables. 'Why are we here, do I need to apologise again'? Hannah thought to herself.

The car soon came to a halt and Hannah saw Ruth and Tilly standing in the yard talking. She hopped out of the car looking around, but the stables looked the same as it always did; the horses happily munching the grass out in the paddocks, the ménage with rays of sun shining down and the chickens pecking away at the old corn.

It was then Hannah heard a faint low whinny; she swirled around and scanned the area; she was certain that was the little wild pony. She decided she was being silly and began to walk towards Ruth and Tilly, who had huge smiles across their faces.

'What's going on?' Hannah muttered, confused as to why she had been brought to stables when it wasn't a Saturday. She heard another low whinny, this time clearer and louder, almost demanding and she was certain someone was either playing a trick on her, or the little wild pony was close by somewhere.

'Well, before he screams my yard down you best go look in the stables, Hannah!' Ruth shouted, and Tilly giggled while Hannah's parents watched her expression change as she figured out what Ruth meant.

Hannah stared at Ruth for a long time, before turning around and bolting for the stables. 'It couldn't be, could it?' Hannah sprinted across the yard. She slowly crept into the stables, almost pinching herself, wondering if this was all a dream. Her questions were soon answered, as the little wild pony let out another whinny...

Chapter Twelve

Hannah still couldn't believe it as she crouched down next to the little pony; it was almost as if they were reliving the steps from the previous day. Hannah held her hand out wanting to touch the little ball of fuzz, and was surprised as the little pony nuzzled her. She blinked back the tears, so happy that the little pony was here.

'Well would you look at that, this little fella wouldn't let us near him at all today, we had to herd him into the stable!' said Ruth, now standing outside the stable with Tilly and Hannah's parents.

'Where did you find him?' Hannah asked, as she gently stroked the tiny pony.

'He followed the trail of carrots after all' replied Tilly, who was now beaming with happiness as she looked at Hannah.

'This really is a fairy tale, I can't believe it!' Hannah laughed.

Hannah's parents were so happy to see Hannah back to her usual self as they had been quite worried about her lately.

'Were so sorry we didn't believe you' said her Mum.

Hannah nodded 'I suppose it does sound a bit silly doesn't it, coming home and saying I've seen a wild pony' replied Hannah. The group began to giggle.

'Have you thought of any names yet then, Hannah?' asked Dad.

'Hmm, I was thinking that maybe Little Alf would be a good name, because he is so cute, and fluffy, and so so tiny, and I just love him so much already.' replied Hannah as she stroked Little Alf.

'Welcome to the family then, Little Alf!' said Hannah's Dad happily.

Look out for the next book to discover the real magic of little Alf... ★

About the Author

Hannah Louise Russell published her first book in 2014, 'The magical adventure of little Alf – The discovery of the wild pony.'

At the young age of 17 years old.

Hannah Russell is the owner of Little Alf who happily lives behind her house in the North Yorkshire Dales and is usually found creating mischief in his home .

The reason Hannah decided to write a series on little Alf is because he is completely different from other miniature Shetlands, as he is a mini mini mini mini Shetland due to little Alf having dwarfism, therefore this makes little Alf super tiny, as well as being super cute!

Hannah and little Alf have a very special bond and are never found far apart.

Little Alf brings Hannah great happiness and joy and hopes he will to other people to as they experience the magic of little Alf....

H.L.Russell & little Alf

X

Follow Little Alf's Blog to see what mischief he is up to recently:

http://itslittlealf.tumblr.com/

Or

'Like 'us on Face book under

'Hannah Russell Author'

Little Alf helps support the RDA- Riding for disabled association.

The RDA, helps horses and ponies provide therapy, achievement and enjoyment to people with disabilities all over the UK.

The RDA have a network of 500 volunteer groups organise activities such as riding, carriage driving, vaulting and show jumping to up to 28,000 people each year.

The RDA has been carrying out life changing activities for over 40 years, and takes great pride in the exceptional standard of their instructors and volunteers.

Little Alf & Hannah are helping support the RDA through their books, every time a book sells a donation goes towards the RDA.

You can find out more information on the RDA website:

http://www.rda.org.uk/

Little AH helps support the RDA - Riding for disabled association

The RDA, helps horses and ponies provide therapy, achievement and enjoyment to people with disabilities all over the UK

The RDA have a network of 500 volunteer groups organise activities such as riding, carriage driving, vaulting and show jumping to up to 28,000 people each year.

The RDA has been carrying out life changing activity for over 40 years, and takes great pride in the exceptional standard of their instructors and volunteers.

Little AH & Hannah are helping support the RDA through their books, every time a book sells a donation goes towards the RDA

You can find out more information on the RDA's website.